STORIES OF THE BIBLE

STORIES OF THE BIBLE **Christmas**
 Drejervej 15,3 DK-2400 Copenhagen NV, Denmark
Tel.: (+45) 3531 0330 Fax: (+45) 3531 0334
E-mail: info@scanpublishing.dk
Website: www.scanpublishing.dk

Design by Ben Alex
Printed in China
ISBN 87 7247 772 5 (Hard cover)
ISBN 87 7247 768 7 (Soft cover)

STORIES OF THE BIBLE

CHRISTMAS

Luke 2:1—21

Illustrations by
Gustavo Mazali

scandinavia

A special baby

One day an angel came to Mary and told her she was going to have a baby. "This is a very special baby," the angel said. "His name shall be Jesus and he will be the Son of God!"

As soon as the angel had left, Mary ran home to Joseph, her husband-to-be, and told him what the angel had said.

No room at the inn

Mary and Joseph were on their way to Bethlehem, a city far away. Mary was pregnant and was soon to have her baby. But when they finally came to Bethlehem, there was no room for them at the inn.

Born in a barn

The inn keeper told Mary and Joseph they could stay in the barn for the night.

This very night Jesus was born. God's own Son was born among cows and sheep in a barn in Bethlehem!

Shepherds in the field

In a field nearby, some shepherds were taking care of their sheep. Suddenly they heard singing, and as they looked up, the sky was filled with angels! The angels told the shepherds the good news that the Son of God had been born in Bethlehem.

Three wise men

Far away in the East, some wise men heard of Jesus' birth. They thought that Jesus must be a king and set out to see him. They followed the bright star all the way to Bethlehem until they came to the house where Jesus was.

Gifts to Baby Jesus

The shepherds and the wise men were very happy.
They knew this baby was the Son of God.
The wise men brought gifts to Jesus to show how grateful they were to God.

The first Christmas in the Bible

In those days Caesar Augustus issued a decree that a census should be taken of the entire Roman world. (This was the first census that took place while Quirinius was governor of Syria.) And everyone went to his own town to register.

So Joseph also went up from the town of Nazareth in Galilee to Judea, to Bethlehem the town of David, because he belonged to the house and line of David. He went there to register with Mary, who was pledged to be married to him and was expecting a child. While they were there, the time came for the baby to be born, and she gave birth to her firstborn, a son. She wrapped him in cloths and placed him in a manger, because there was no room for them in the inn.

Luke 2:1-7